*For my daughters, Amelia and Julia,
whose curiosity and love of learning fill me
with endless joy and pride*

KITCHEN SCIENCE FOR TODDLERS

Kitchen Science for Toddlers

20 Edible STEAM Activities and Experiments to Enjoy!

Melissa Mazur

Illustrations by Natascha Rosenberg

ROCKRIDGE PRESS

Interior and Cover Designer: Diana Haas
Art Producer: Samantha Ulban
Editor: Alyson Penn
Production Editor: Matthew Burnett
Production Manager: Jose Olivera

Illustrations © 2021 Natascha Rosenberg.
Author photograph courtesy of Emily Parish Photography. Illustrator photograph courtesy of Cesar Montegrifo.

ISBN: Print 978-1-63807-114-3 | eBook 978-1-63807-165-5
R0

Contents

To the Grown-Ups

This book contains 20 STEAM-based kitchen activities that encourage learning through play. STEAM stands for science, technology, engineering, art, and mathematics, and it is an educational approach to learning that integrates these subjects to help guide student inquiry and critical thinking. Because the kitchen is often the center of the home, it's the perfect place to introduce learning activities. Children are also curious by nature, especially when it comes to food and how things work. My own daughters love pretending they're little scientists, whipping up "experiments" and observing chemical and physical changes in the kitchen.

The benefits of involving kids in the kitchen are plentiful. They will gain a willingness to try new things, develop a sense of pride, and grow in their independence, and they'll develop curiosity, fine motor skills, and an extended attention span. Most important, they will spend quality time and build lasting memories with the people they love.

This book contains STEAM activities especially tailored for toddlers. The hands-on learning activities help equip children with the skills and knowledge necessary to become 21st-century citizens and solve real-world problems. It is never too early to start developing these skills!

While completing the activities in this book, it is important to let children do as much of each activity on their own as safely possible. You are there to assist and facilitate learning. Children gain so much more learning through the trial and error that comes with independence.

In a 2013 study by Mizrap Bulunuz ("Teaching Science Through Play in Kindergarten: Does Integrated Play and Science Instruction Build Understanding?"), researchers investigated "kindergarten children's understanding of science concepts when experiencing science through play versus direct instruction." They concluded that "children with the same demographics who participated in teaching science through play made significantly greater gains in learning of science concepts than the children who experienced the didactic teaching approach."

Parents are a child's first teachers. You have a vital role in supporting your child's learning and development, and doing so with a play-based approached provides opportunities for bonding, communication, and inspiring a love of science.

As an educator starting out in upper elementary education and later transitioning to a role as a preschool science and technology teacher, I've had the wonderful opportunity to see just how curious young minds are. It was always very encouraging for me to see that, through play-based learning, toddlers are extremely capable of understanding many of the same concepts that my older students were expected to master. Their inquisitive natures and growing minds have shown me that toddlers really can do and comprehend much more than we think!

This book offers science activities that have specific learning outcomes. Many of the activities are "taste safe," meaning your child will be able to eat at least one part of the end result. You may guide your child on what they can safely taste and what they can't. You know your child best and can set the limits on what is best for them. It would be wonderful to include your child in the process of choosing an activity. Look through the book with your child, and read aloud the activities or descriptions. Set a time in the future when you can do the activity together. At the beginning of each activity, you will find a Messy Meter as well as the average time to complete it and flags for any possible allergens used. At the end of the activities, you will find Prep Ahead, Substitutions, Fun Together, and Tricky Tips. These tips will give you all the information you need to successfully complete the activities in the book. Be sure to read them before you get started.

To make the most out of the time together with your child, plan to do the activity when you aren't in a rush. Most activities take 15 to 30 minutes to complete, so be sure to carve out enough time not only to do the activity but to set up and clean up. Allow your child the freedom to taste safe ingredients (no raw eggs). You may also encourage them to smell and touch things along the way.

I urge you to let your child take the lead in safe steps, especially with measuring, mixing, and pouring. Provide your child with opportunities to complete tasks that they can reasonably accomplish. Ask a lot of questions, such as: What do you see happening? What do you think might happen next? What does it feel (or sound, smell, or taste) like? Most important, have fun and enjoy yourselves as you cook up some kitchen science!

To the Kid Scientists

This book was written just for you. I know how much you love helping in the kitchen and how curious you are. With these 20 activities, you'll have fun and discover new things at the same time.

As you experiment with the activities in this book, you will be testing out what's called "the scientific method," just like real scientists do.

You will choose what to research.
You will carefully work through each experiment.
You will report what happened during the experiment.

As a scientist, it's your job to ask a lot of questions and make many observations. An observation is when you look at, or observe, something very carefully to see what is happening. Watch carefully during each step of your experiments so you don't miss any changes that might happen.

Most important of all, have fun!

PART 1
PREPARE FOR PLAY

Kitchen Lab Rules

Safety is the most important ingredient in any activity. Here are some basic rules to follow to ensure that everyone has fun and stays safe in the kitchen.

ALWAYS HAVE AN ADULT HELP.

Adults should supervise all kitchen activities. However, certain steps—such as using the oven or cutting food into small pieces—should only ever be done by an adult. The "Just for adults" text will let you know when to ask your grown-up for help.

WASH YOUR HANDS.

Even little hands can carry a lot of germs! A big part of kitchen safety is washing your hands with soap and water. Lather up while singing "Twinkle, Twinkle, Little Star," and then rinse well with warm water.

WASH YOUR INGREDIENTS.

It's important to wash all fruits and vegetables under running water to remove any bacteria, dirt, or pesticides. You may even want to use a brush to scrub firm produce. Properly cleaning foods helps protect us from foodborne illnesses.

HANDLE FOOD SAFELY.

Remember to wash your hands *before and after* doing these science activities, especially after handling eggs. Use separate utensils and bowls for raw eggs, and clean these surfaces immediately after use. Never eat foods that contain raw eggs, such as dough or meringue, before they are cooked.

ORGANIZE YOUR WORK SPACE.

Before you begin any activity, gather all of your supplies and ingredients. (Everything you need is listed at the beginning of each experiment.) Make sure all surfaces are clean and sharp objects are out of reach.

CLEAN UP AS YOU GO.

Cleaning up is always easier if you do it as you go. If something spills, wipe it up right away. After using bowls and utensils, place them in the sink so they don't get in your way. When you're finished using knives, put them away out of reach.

SAFETY FIRST!

All of the science activities included in this book are designed for a toddler to do with a supervising adult. While each of the activities is fairly simple, there are still a few basic rules to follow to keep everyone happy and healthy in the kitchen lab.

- Cut food into bite-size pieces before serving it to a child, especially known choking hazards such as grapes and apples.

- Be mindful of all ingredients included in each activity to avoid triggering food allergies. Replace allergens with ingredients that are safe for your child to touch or consume.

- Please be aware of potential dangers when it comes to sharp objects and kitchen equipment. When they are not in use, put away any knives or other sharp objects.

- Before using electric mixers, remind your child about the importance of keeping hands and fingers outside the bowl. Turn off and unplug the electric mixer once it is no longer needed.

- When using the oven, a supervising adult should take the cooked item out and place it in an area out of reach until it has cooled.

- Be sure to take down and put away the kitchen lab setup after the science activity has been finished.

Kid Scientist Tools

In order to complete the activities in this book, you will need some common kitchen items. See how many of the items in the following lists your child knows, and teach them the names of any items they may not be familiar with.

Tools & Utensils

Jars or cups (glass or plastic)

Knives (for adult use)

Mixing spoons

Plates and bowls (glass or plastic)

Resealable bags (gallon and sandwich sizes)

Small cups (glass, plastic, or paper)

Spatula

Toothpicks

Cookware & Bakeware

Baking sheet

Cookie cutters

Hand mixer

Measuring cups/spoons

Pizza pan

Other Stuff

Paintbrushes

Pipe cleaners

Spray bottle/pipette/medicine dropper

Before You Begin

Each science activity in this book uses a variety of ingredients and kitchen tools. The science activities are designed to be completed together with your child. Taking a little time to prepare in advance will make for an engaging and quality learning experience.

Read over each experiment prior to starting it with your kid scientist. Some activities require brief preparations beforehand. Look for the special tips (after each set of instructions) to help the activity run smoothly. The science behind each activity is also explained in the "How It Works" section—use it to explain the experiment to your child and answer any questions they might have.

Designate a specific area of your kitchen for your "lab." Set out all the ingredients and tools before beginning each activity to reduce the amount of downtime and potential distractions for your child.

Some activities require measuring out ingredients. Kids love using measuring spoons and cups in the kitchen. Ask them to pour and carefully measure the ingredients over a separate bowl to catch any potential spills.

Most important, always practice kitchen safety. Discuss kitchen rules before each science activity (see page 2). Explain how to use kitchen tools safely and correctly. Let your child know ahead of time which parts if any, they can eat at the end of each experiment.

PART 2
TASTE THE SCIENCE

Baking Soda Fizzy Paint

Bring your artwork to life! Watch your picture erupt with tiny fizzing bubbles when you paint with baking soda and vinegar.

Science Question What happens when you combine baking soda and vinegar?

MESSY METER: 4

TIME NEEDED: 20 minutes

ALLERGY ALERT: None

WHAT YOU NEED

Apron, smock, or old T-shirt to protect clothing, if desired

¼ dry measuring cup

¾ cup baking soda

3 small plastic or paper cups

Liquid measuring cup

¾ cup water

Whisk or fork for mixing

Red, yellow, and blue food coloring

Paintbrush

White cardstock

Pipette, medicine dropper, or spray bottle

¼ cup white vinegar

1. Make your paint: Using the dry measuring cup, carefully measure out ¼ cup of baking soda and put it in one of the cups.

2. Using the liquid measuring cup, measure out ¼ cup of water and add it to the same cup. Stir it well with a whisk or fork.

3. Carefully add 2 to 3 drops of red food coloring to the liquid mixture. Stir well.

4. Repeat steps 1 through 3 using both the yellow and blue food coloring so you end up with three different cups of paint.

5. It's time to paint! Dip the paintbrush into the colored water (stir if the baking soda has settled to the bottom) and paint onto a piece of cardstock.

6. Now make your painting come alive. Fill a spray bottle with the vinegar or use a cup and medicine dropper. Spray or drop vinegar onto your painting and watch the chemical reaction bring your painting to life!

continued ›

SPECIAL TIPS

Prep ahead: Make cleanup easier by placing the cardstock on a tray or baking sheet.

Fun together: Before you mix the baking soda with water, ask your child what they think that powder is. Do they say sugar or flour? They can touch it to see what it feels like and take a small taste of it on their finger.

Tricky tips: Remember, don't let the baking soda settle to the bottoms of the cups. For the best reaction, keep your paint well mixed.

HOW IT WORKS

When baking soda (a base) and vinegar (an acid) are combined, a chemical reaction occurs. The bubbles that are produced are filled with carbon dioxide gas.

MY SCIENTIST LIKED

_____

_____

_____

Matter Floats

Observe the three states of matter—solid, liquid, and gas—while you make and enjoy a delicious root beer float.

Science Question What happens when you mix ice cream with root beer?

MESSY METER: 1

TIME NEEDED: 10 minutes

ALLERGY ALERT: Dairy

~~~~~

WHAT YOU NEED

For each float:

Ice-cream scoop or large spoon

2 scoops vanilla ice cream

Clear cup or mug

Liquid measuring cup

1 cup regular or caffeine-free root beer

Spoon for mixing

Straw

1. Place 2 scoops of ice cream into a clear cup or mug.

2. Using a liquid measuring cup, measure out 1 cup of root beer. Carefully pour it on top of the ice cream.

3. Using a spoon, gently mix the root beer and ice cream. Watch what happens. How many layers do you see?

4. It's time to eat your experiment! Enjoy your root beer float with a straw and a spoon.

continued ›

SPECIAL TIPS

Prep ahead: Make the mug extra cold and frosty by placing it in the freezer for up to an hour before making the root beer float.

Substitutions: This experiment works equally well with dairy-free ice cream. You can also use orange soda, grape soda, or cola instead of root beer.

Fun together: Which of the two ingredients is a liquid? (Answer: root beer) Which is a solid? (Answer: ice cream) What are the bubbles? (Answer: a gas)

HOW IT WORKS

When you mix together the solid (ice cream) and liquid (root beer), they react and create a foamy layer of bubbles. These bubbles trap the carbonation (the gas) already present in the root beer, so you can see all three states of matter (solid, liquid, gas) in one place.

MY SCIENTIST LIKED

_____

_____

_____

Rainbow Lettuce

Have you ever wondered how a plant drinks water? This colorful investigation shows you how.

Science Question What happens when you put lettuce leaves in colored water?

MESSY METER: 2

TIME NEEDED: 40 minutes

ALLERGY ALERT: Nuts (see "Substitutions" tip)

WHAT YOU NEED

Apron, smock, or old T-shirt to protect clothing, if desired

4 clear glass or plastic cups

Water

Red, yellow, green, and blue food coloring

Spoon for mixing

4 leaves of romaine lettuce or cabbage

1. Fill each of the clear cups with water, leaving about an inch of space at the top.

2. To each cup, add 15 to 20 drops of food coloring so you end up with 4 different cups of colored water. Using a spoon, stir each well.

3. Wash the lettuce. Place one leaf of lettuce into each cup so that the lettuce sticks up out of the cup. Now it's time to wait for the science to happen. Let the lettuce soak in the colored water for about 30 minutes.

4. After about 30 minutes, observe what happened to the lettuce leaves.

5. It's time to eat your experiment! Cut the lettuce into small pieces, add your favorite toppings and dressing, and enjoy a rainbow salad.

continued ›

SPECIAL TIPS

Prep ahead: Choose lettuce leaves that are light in color. The "heart" leaves, or leaves toward the middle of the bunch, are generally paler.

Substitutions: You can use celery stalks with leaves instead of lettuce. To enjoy, fill your colored celery with your favorite nut or no-nut butter.

Fun together: Which part of the lettuce is the most colorful? Look at the bottom of the lettuce. What do you see? Peel open the lettuce stalk to see what it looks like inside.

Tricky tips: Darker-colored water produces more colorful leaves, so make sure the water is very saturated with color. The longer you leave the lettuce in water, the more colorful it will become.

HOW IT WORKS

Plants move the water in the soil to their branches and leaves through their roots. The process is called "capillary action."

MY SCIENTIST LIKED

_____

_____

_____

Fruit Density

Density refers to how much mass or matter an object contains. Learn about the density of different fruits with this sweet science activity—all you need is a bowl of water and your favorite fruits!

Science Question Which fruits will sink in water, and which will float?

MESSY METER: 1

TIME NEEDED: 10 minutes

ALLERGY ALERT: None

WHAT YOU NEED

Medium clear bowl

4 cups water

1 orange

1 grape

1 apple

1 strawberry

1 cherry

1 blueberry

5 tablespoons table salt

Tablespoon

1. Fill a clear bowl with the water.

2. Choose a fruit to try first. Do you think it will sink or float?

3. Carefully place the fruit in the water. Use your observation skills: Does the fruit sink or float? What can we tell about the density of the fruit if it sinks? How about if it floats?

4. Repeat this experiment with each of the remaining fruits. Which fruits sank, and which fruits floated?

5. Now add the salt, 1 tablespoon at a time, to the bowl of water. After adding each spoonful, stir until the salt has dissolved. Drop in one blueberry. How does it behave in the water now? Has its density changed?

6. It's time to eat your experiment! Take the fruit out of the water. Rinse it well under running water. Ask your adult to cut any extra fruit into pieces to make a fruit salad. Enjoy!

continued ›

SPECIAL TIPS

Substitutions: This experiment can be done with any fruits. Try kiwi, raspberries, or lemons. Even a watermelon might surprise you! Just make sure to have a few different types on hand so you have several examples of sinking and floating.

Fun together: Place an orange both with and without the peel in the water—how does peeling the orange change what happens? What happens when we add salt to the water? What can we do to make the grape and cherry float?

Tricky tips: The amount of salt you need to add depends on how much water you have in the bowl. If you aren't noticing a difference with the blueberries, for example, try stirring in more salt one tablespoon at a time.

HOW IT WORKS

Fruit will float or sink depending on its density. Fruits with a lot of air pockets inside are less dense than water and will float. Adding salt to water makes the water denser, which means that your fruit also has a greater chance of floating.

MY SCIENTIST LIKED

_____

_____

_____

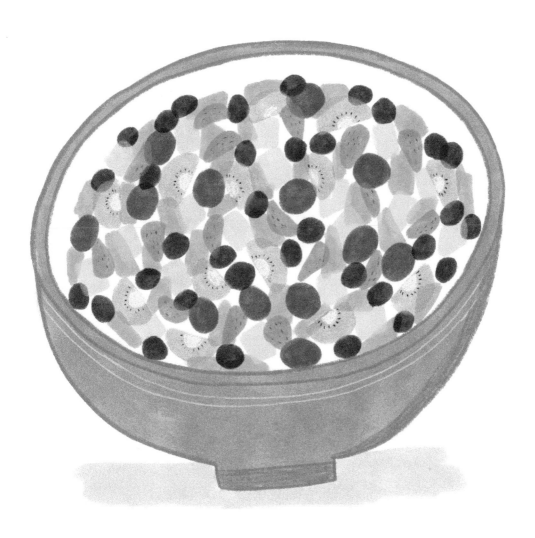

Eggshell Planters

Recycle eggshells into little pots to grow plants in! These charming little egg planters are perfect for observing seeds as they begin to sprout.

Science Question How does an eggshell help plants grow?

MESSY METER: 3

TIME NEEDED: Overnight to soak beans; 20 minutes to prepare eggshell pots; several days for beans to sprout

ALLERGY ALERT: Egg

WHAT YOU NEED

Butter knife

6 eggs

1 egg carton

Soil

6 dried pinto beans or lima beans, soaked overnight

Water

1. **Just for adults:** Using a butter knife, carefully crack the tops off the eggs, pouring the egg yolks and whites into a bowl. Cover the bowl of eggs and refrigerate it until you are ready to cook them. Make an omelette or scrambled eggs after your experiment!

2. Rinse the eggshells well under lukewarm water. Be careful not to crack the eggshells; these will be the pots for your dirt and seeds. Place the rinsed eggshells in the egg carton.

3. Time to get your hands dirty! Fill each of the eggshells three-quarters full with soil. Place your eggshell planters back into the egg carton so they sit upright. Press one pre-soaked bean into the soil of each planter. Cover the bean with more soil.

4. Water the soil. Place the egg carton near a sunny window. Now it's time to wait for your beans to grow. (It can take several days to see sprouts, so be patient!)

5. Once the beans sprout and form more than two leaves, you can transfer the seedlings into the garden: Dig holes a little larger than your egg pots. Gently crack each eggshell pot to give the roots of the plant space to grow. Then place the egg-shell pots into the holes so the top of each pot is level with the ground. Fill the holes with soil. Water and watch your plants grow bigger in the coming days. In a couple months, you'll be able to eat fresh beans from your own garden!

continued ›

SPECIAL TIPS

Prep ahead: Soak beans in water for at least 8 hours prior to planting.

Fun together: Draw silly faces on the eggshells before you crack them. Plant several different types of beans or seeds to see which will sprout the quickest. Don't forget to cook the eggs!

Tricky tips: To crack just the top off an egg, use a butter knife to gently tap on the shell and make a small hole. Then pick away the pieces of shell with your fingers.

HOW IT WORKS

Eggshells contain calcium and are a great fertilizer. Once planted, the eggshell will naturally decompose and provide nutrients to your beans as they grow.

MY SCIENTIST LIKED

_____

_____

_____

Homemade Lava Lamp

Make your own groovy lava lamp at home using oil, water, and Alka-Seltzer.

Science Question What happens when you mix oil, water, and Alka-Seltzer?

MESSY METER: 1

TIME NEEDED: 10 minutes

ALLERGY ALERT: None

WHAT YOU NEED

Large jar or clear glass

Water

Vegetable oil

Food coloring (your choice of color)

Alka-Seltzer tablet

1. Fill the jar one-quarter full with water.

2. Add enough vegetable oil so the jar is three-quarters full of liquid.

3. Add 8 to 10 drops of food coloring to the liquid.

4. Break an Alka-Seltzer tablet in half and drop one half into the liquid.

5. Watch what happens! After the bubbles stop, you can add the other half of the Alka-Seltzer tablet to restart them.

6. If you are hungry, use any leftover vegetable oil, toss with some vegetables— broccoli, carrots, green beans—and roast them in the oven at 400°F for about 20 minutes for a healthy snack.

continued ›

SPECIAL TIPS

Fun together: Before you add the Alka-Seltzer, observe what is happening inside the jar. Add the tablet. What do you hear now? How do you think the little bubbles move?

Tricky tips: Each Alka-Seltzer tablet should last a few minutes. You only need to use half of one at a time to get the desired effect. A note on cleanup: Do not pour the oil mixture down the drain—it could clog the sink. Pour it outside.

HOW IT WORKS

Water and oil do not mix. Bubbles caused by the Alka-Seltzer tablet stick to small drops of oil and carry them to the top of the jar. When the bubbles pop, the oil sinks back to the bottom.

MY SCIENTIST LIKED

_____

_____

_____

Butterfly Life Cycle Snack

Have you ever wondered how a caterpillar becomes a butterfly? Make this delicious snack to learn all about this beautiful insect's life cycle.

Science Question How does a caterpillar change?

MESSY METER: 2

TIME NEEDED: 15 minutes

ALLERGY ALERT:

Dairy, Gluten

WHAT YOU NEED

A knife

1 stalk of celery with leaves on top

12 raisins, divided

2 grapes

2 pretzel sticks or twists

1 tortilla wrap

1 string cheese, cut in half

4 slices of a mandarin orange

Plate

1. Make stage 1 of your butterfly's life cycle: the egg. Place 2 celery leaves on a plate. Arrange 6 raisins on top of the leaves. The raisins are your caterpillar eggs.

2. Make stage 2 of your butterfly's life cycle: the caterpillar. **Just for adults:** Using a knife, cut a 2- to 3-inch piece of celery stalk. Place it round-side up on the plate. This will be your caterpillar's body. To make a head, place a grape at one end of the celery. Add a piece of pretzel on either side of the grape to make antennae. Give your caterpillar feet by arranging 6 raisins along the bottom of the celery stalk.

3. Make stage 3 of your butterfly's life cycle: the chrysalis. Place a tortilla wrap on a clean work surface. Place half of a string cheese on the tortilla. Fold in each side of the tortilla, and then fold the bottom upward and keep rolling the tortilla into a tight package. This is your chrysalis.

4. Make stage 4 of your butterfly's life cycle: the butterfly. Place the remaining half of the string cheese on the plate. This will be your butterfly's body. Add a grape on top for a head, mandarin oranges for wings, and pretzel pieces for antennae. Congratulations! You've just completed a butterfly's entire life cycle, from egg to beautiful butterfly. It's time to eat your snack!

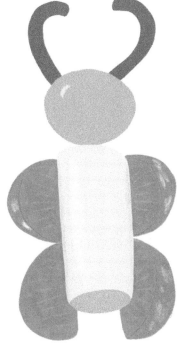

continued ›

SPECIAL TIPS

Substitutions: You can use dairy-free (vegan) string cheese or substitute additional pieces of celery for the string cheese.

Fun together: What else do you have in your refrigerator that looks like the parts of a butterfly or caterpillar? Use different foods to make a new version of the butterfly life cycle snack.

HOW IT WORKS

A butterfly's life cycle starts when a female butterfly lays her eggs on the leaves or stems of plants. Each egg will hatch a larva, or caterpillar. The larva will then transform into a pupa, also called a chrysalis. A chrysalis is the hard shell covering a caterpillar as it transforms into a butterfly. When the caterpillar has transformed, it emerges as an adult butterfly.

MY SCIENTIST LIKED

_____

_____

_____

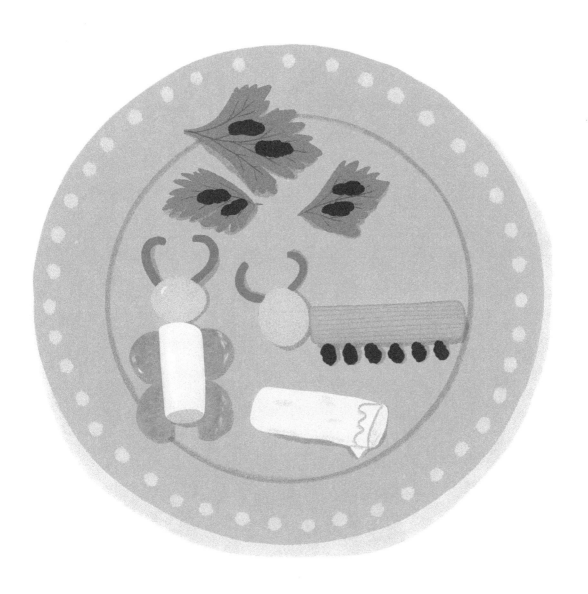

Baby Food Playdough

Making your own playdough is fun and easy! Use baby food to add a delicious scent and natural food coloring to your homemade dough.

Science Question How can you use food to make playdough?

MESSY METER: 4

TIME NEEDED: 30 minutes

ALLERGY ALERT: Gluten

WHAT YOU NEED

Apron, smock, or old T-shirt to protect clothing, if desired

Dry measuring cup

1 cup all-purpose flour

Large bowl

1 cup cornstarch

Spoon for mixing

Measuring spoons

3 tablespoons vegetable oil

4-ounce pouch of baby food

Tools for playing with the dough: rolling pin, cookie cutters, potato masher

1. Using the dry measuring cup, carefully measure out 1 cup of flour. Put it in the bowl. Next, measure out 1 cup of cornstarch. Add it to the bowl. Mix well with the spoon.

2. Using a measuring spoon, carefully measure out 3 tablespoons of vegetable oil. Add it to the flour mixture. Then add the baby food. Stir well with a spoon until the mixture comes together.

3. Turn the dough out onto a clean work surface. Using your hands, knead the dough until it is well combined and soft.

4. Your playdough is now ready to play with! Try cutting out shapes with cookie cutters or making patterns with a potato masher. Have fun!

5. Store your playdough in a resealable bag or airtight container.

continued ›

SPECIAL TIPS

Substitutions: To make gluten-free playdough, substitute an equal amount of rice cereal for the flour.

Fun together: For fun, purchase a few different types of baby food. Set up a baby food taste-test. Cover your child's eyes and have him or her guess the flavor.

Tricky tips: If the mixture is too dry, add more vegetable oil ½ tablespoon at a time. For best results, use bright-colored baby food such as beets, peas, or carrots as a natural food dye. If you'd like to make your dough more vibrant, you can add a few drops of food coloring to the vegetable oil before mixing it with the dry ingredients.

HOW IT WORKS

By adding the wet ingredients (vegetable oil and baby food) to the dry ingredients (flour and cornstarch), you change the consistency of the ingredients. After kneading, the ingredients turn into a dough that you can mold or roll out into shapes.

MY SCIENTIST LIKED

_____

_____

_____

Transforming Milk into Plastic

Is it possible to make a solid by mixing two liquids? You bet. Discover how you can make plastic by mixing milk and vinegar!

Science Question What happens when you add vinegar to hot milk?

MESSY METER: 3

TIME NEEDED: 15 minutes; 48 hours to dry

ALLERGY ALERT: Dairy

WHAT YOU NEED

2 cups milk

Medium bowls

Measuring spoon

8 teaspoons white vinegar

Spoon

Paper towels

Plate

Small cookie cutters

String

1. Pour 2 cups of milk into a bowl. Microwave until hot, about 2 minutes. Taste the milk for a warm treat.

2. Into a separate bowl, measure 8 teaspoons of vinegar. Add the hot milk to the vinegar.

3. Mix the milk and vinegar with a spoon until you see white curds.

4. Place several layers of paper towels on a plate. Scoop the curds onto the paper towels.

5. Use the paper towels to press out excess moisture from the curds.

6. Knead until smooth. Press flat and use cookie cutters to cut shapes. Poke holes and let dry for 48 hours. Thread the shapes onto a string to wear as a necklace or use as counters for math.

continued ›

SPECIAL TIPS

Fun together: Add food coloring to the milk to make your plastic colorful. Alternatively, you can color the white plastic shapes with markers after they dry. After adding the vinegar, ask, "What is happening to the milk?" While kneading, ask, "How does this feel?"

HOW IT WORKS

When adding vinegar (an acid) to milk, a protein in the milk begins to coagulate and turn into curds. These curds are casein, which is used to create glue and plastic.

MY SCIENTIST LIKED

_____

_____

_____

Melon Tower of Strength

Build a tower using melon cubes and toothpicks. How tall and sturdy can you make it?

Science Question What shape of melon tower is the sturdiest?

MESSY METER: 2

TIME NEEDED: 20 minutes

ALLERGY ALERT: None

WHAT YOU NEED

1 watermelon

1 cantaloupe

1 honeydew melon

3 medium bowls

Baking sheet

1 box of toothpicks

Tape measure

A fork

1. **Just for adults:** Cut the watermelon, cantaloupe, and honeydew melon into 15 cubes each. Place the cubes of each type of melon into separate bowls.

2. Time to build! Place three different melon cubes on a baking sheet. Using toothpicks, stack the cubes on top of one another to build a short tower.

3. Now, build an even higher tower. Add three more melon cubes, using toothpicks to fasten them in place.

4. Continue stacking cubes and using toothpicks to build your tower as high as you can without it falling over.

5. Using the tape measure, measure the height of your tower.

6. Now disassemble your tower. Repeat steps 2 to 5, but this time build your tower with a big square base. How high did you get this time? Now try something different: Repeat steps 2 to 5, but this time build your tower with a triangular base. How does changing the shape of the base affect your tower?

7. It's time to eat your experiment! Enjoy eating your tower block by block.

continued ›

SPECIAL TIPS

Prep ahead: Pre-cut the melon before beginning the activity with your child.

Fun together: Make a few different types of structures. Which one is the sturdiest? Which was the easiest to build? Which was the tallest? Instead of toothpicks, try using Greek yogurt as "mortar" between the melon bricks.

Tricky tips: Stacking one melon on top of the other will allow you to build a tall tower quickly, but it might not be stable. Try creating a square base and build on that. Guide your child and allow them to experiment.

HOW IT WORKS

Your child will discover, through trial and error, that structures with large bases tend to be stronger and more stable.

MY SCIENTIST LIKED

_____

_____

_____

Create a Rainbow

In this activity, you will learn about the colors of a rainbow and how they are created—and then eat them!

Science Question What colors are in a rainbow?

MESSY METER: 2
TIME NEEDED: 15 minutes
ALLERGY ALERT: Gluten

WHAT YOU NEED

1 small bowl

Fruity loops cereal

Picture of a rainbow

Pipe cleaner

2 powdered donuts

1. Fill the bowl with cereal.

2. Now, look at a picture of a rainbow. What colors do you see? Be sure to notice in what order the colors appear.

3. Now it's time to build your own rainbow. Take 3 pieces of each color of cereal out of the bowl and place them on the table.

4. Look at the picture of the rainbow. Take the red cereal pieces and thread them onto your pipe cleaner.

5. Repeat with the remaining cereal. Be sure to follow the order of colors shown on your rainbow picture. Leave about 1 inch of pipe cleaner exposed on both ends.

6. Carefully place each exposed end of the pipe cleaner into the hole of one donut so that your rainbow is arched. Congratulations! You just made your very own edible rainbow. Celebrate by eating everything but the pipe cleaner as a snack.

continued ›

SPECIAL TIPS

Substitutions: You can substitute jumbo marshmallows for the powdered donuts, if you like.

Fun together: After this activity, make your own real rainbow! Go outside and stand in a spot where the sun is behind you. Turn on the hose and place your thumb over the nozzle so the water sprays. Watch a rainbow appear!

HOW IT WORKS

Sunlight looks white, but it's really made up of several beams of colors: red, orange, yellow, green, blue, indigo, and violet. A rainbow is made when sunlight passes through raindrops. The raindrops bend the light, making it look like arches of different colors. The colors in a real rainbow are similar to the colors in the cereal.

MY SCIENTIST LIKED

_____

_____

_____

Celery Ramp

Discover some principles of physics as you learn how to adjust the incline of a ramp in this fun target game.

Science Question How does the incline of a ramp impact how far something will travel?

MESSY METER: 2

TIME NEEDED: 15 minutes

ALLERGY ALERT: Dairy

WHAT YOU NEED

Large table

5 pieces of cereal (Cheerios work well)

Colored tape

1 stalk of celery

2 yogurt-covered raisins

1. Working at one side of a table, arrange 5 pieces of cereal in different spots. On the other side of the table, fasten a small piece of colored tape.

2. Now, get your celery. Hold it so that the thick end rests on the tape. Hold up the smaller end to make a ramp.

3. Place a yogurt-covered raisin at the top of your celery ramp and let it slide down. Try to hit one of the pieces of cereal on the table.

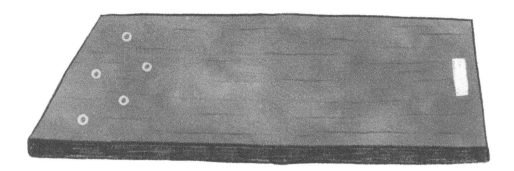

4. Now that you have the hang of your ramp, it's time to experiment. Try turning, raising, and lowering your celery to change the incline and direction of the ramp.

5. Roll the yogurt-covered raisins down the celery ramp and try to hit all the targets.

6. After you finish playing with your ramp, it's time to eat your experiment. Enjoy!

continued ›

SPECIAL TIPS

Substitutions: You can use mini marshmallows, plain raisins, blueberries, or other small foods instead of cereal or yogurt-covered raisins.

Fun together: Turn this into a multi-player game! Take turns aiming at a cereal target. Once someone hits a target, they collect that piece of cereal and keep it in a pile. Whoever collects the most pieces of cereal at the end wins!

Tricky tips: For this game, try to select yogurt-covered raisins that are round. They roll better and more evenly down the ramp and across the table.

HOW IT WORKS

As the incline of the celery ramp increases, the raisin will roll faster and farther across the table.

MY SCIENTIST LIKED

_____

_____

_____

Edible Bubbles

Why do some drinks contain fizzing bubbles? How did they get there? Make your own carbonated drink using baking soda.

Science Question What happens when you mix orange juice and baking soda?

MESSY METER: 1

TIME NEEDED: 10 minutes

ALLERGY ALERT: None

WHAT YOU NEED

Liquid measuring cup

1 cup orange juice without pulp

Large clear glass

Teaspoon

1 teaspoon baking soda

Straw

1. Using a liquid measuring cup, carefully measure out 1 cup of orange juice. Pour it into a glass. Take a small sip so you can compare the flavor before and after the experiment.

2. Add 1 teaspoon of baking soda to the orange juice. Stir it until the baking soda dissolves.

3. Now it's time to taste your experiment! Use a straw to take a small sip of your homemade soda.

SPECIAL TIPS

Substitutions: Make sparkling lemonade by using lemonade instead of orange juice.

Fun together: What happened after you added the baking soda? How did the orange juice change? What did it taste like after adding the baking soda?

Tricky tips: Only take a sip or two of your home-made soda. It doesn't taste as good as it did before you added the baking soda.

continued ›

HOW IT WORKS

When the acid from the orange juice (a liquid) mixes with baking soda (a solid), a gas (carbon dioxide) is formed. The bubbles you see are filled with the carbon dioxide.

MY SCIENTIST LIKED

_____

_____

_____

Homemade Butter

Did you know that butter is made from only one ingredient? You won't believe how easy it is to make your own at home. Shake up a batch to find out!

Science Question How does cream turn into butter?

MESSY METER: 1

TIME NEEDED: 15 minutes

ALLERGY ALERT: Dairy

WHAT YOU NEED

Small jar with lid

Heavy (whipping) cream

1. Fill the jar halfway with cream.

2. Screw on the lid tightly.

3. Now it's time to use your muscles! Taking turns with an adult, shake the cream in the jar until it thickens into whipped cream. It will take 5 to 7 minutes. Open the jar and taste the cream.

4. Seal the jar tightly closed again. Continue shaking the jar for another 5 minutes or so, until the cream turns into a solid mass with just a bit of white liquid around it. That mass is your butter!

5. Squeeze any liquid from your butter and pat it dry with a paper towel. Now your experiment is ready to eat! Spread your fresh butter on toast or melt it on hot noodles.

6. Your butter will keep in an airtight container for up to 1 week.

continued ›

Fun together: While the butter is still somewhat soft, you can mold it into fun shapes! You can also add a pinch of salt or a little honey to flavor your butter.

Tricky tips: Shaking takes a lot of energy. You may want to switch who's shaking every minute so you don't get tired. Adding a marble inside the jar will speed up the process. Use a small jar that is easy for little hands to hold.

HOW IT WORKS

Heavy cream contains a lot of fat. When you shake it, the fat molecules in the cream begin to separate from the liquid. They clump together and eventually form solid butter. The liquid you are left with in the jar is buttermilk—you can drink it!

MY SCIENTIST LIKED

_____

_____

_____

Growing Marshmallows

Nothing tastes better than gooey marshmallows roasted over a fire, but what happens when you put marshmallows in the microwave? Heat them for different amounts of time to find out!

Science Question What happens when you microwave marshmallows?

MESSY METER: 2

TIME NEEDED: 10 minutes

ALLERGY ALERT: None

WHAT YOU NEED

5 large marshmallows

5 small microwave-safe plates

1. Place one marshmallow on a plate. Touch it. What does it feel like? Set it aside.

2. Place a second marshmallow on a new plate. **Just for adults:** Heat it in the microwave for 10 seconds. Now, touch the marshmallow. Has it changed?

3. Place a third marshmallow on a different plate. **Just for adults:** Heat it in the microwave for 30 seconds. Touch the marshmallow. What's it look like now?

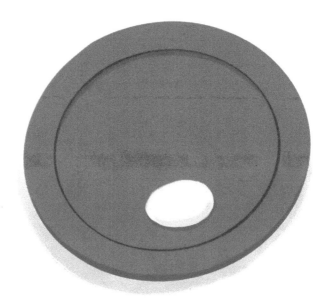

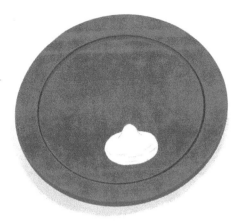

4. Place a fourth marshmallow on a new plate. **Just for adults:** Heat it in the microwave for 60 seconds. Let it cool slightly and then touch it. What's it look like now?

5. Place the fifth marshmallow on a new plate. **Just for adults:** Heat it in the microwave for 2 minutes. Let it cool slightly and then touch it. How would you describe this one?

6. Line up all the plates of marshmallows side by side. Compare what they look and feel like.

7. Now it's time to taste your experiment! Take a small bite from each marshmallow. Do they taste different from one another?

continued ›

SPECIAL TIPS

Fun together: Discuss how the marshmallows look, feel, and taste. Which one do you think tastes the best? What do you think might happen if you heat a marshmallow in the microwave for 5 minutes?

Tricky tips: Show your child the inflated marshmallows as soon as they come out of the microwave and let them continue to watch as the marshmallows begin to shrink as they cool.

HOW IT WORKS

When you heat a marshmallow, the gas inside the marshmallow expands, causing the marshmallow to grow. When it cools, the marshmallow shrinks back down in size.

MY SCIENTIST LIKED

_____

_____

_____

Soil Cups

Have you ever wondered what is under the grass in your yard? Create your own edible treat as you learn about the layers of soil.

Science Question What are the layers of soil?

MESSY METER: 3

TIME NEEDED: 10 minutes

ALLERGY ALERT:

Dairy, Gluten

WHAT YOU NEED

Ingredients:

1 handful of chocolate chips

1 cup chocolate pudding

1 handful of chocolate cookies or graham crackers

2 gummy worms

Equipment:

Clear cup or jar

Spoon

Sandwich baggie

1. Cover the bottom of a cup with a layer of chocolate chips. This layer represents bedrock.

2. Using your spoon, place a thick layer of chocolate pudding on top of the chocolate chip bedrock. This layer represents subsoil.

3. Now it's time to use your muscles! Put some chocolate cookies in a resealable sandwich bag. Seal the bag and, using your hands, crush the cookies into small pieces.

4. Pour the crushed cookies on top of the pudding. This layer represents topsoil.

5. All healthy soil contains worms. To finish, place the gummy worms on top of the cookies.

6. It's time to eat your experiment! Use your spoon as a shovel and dig in.

continued ›

Fun together: As you add layers to the cup, identify each layer and talk about what it contains (see "How It Works," this page).

Tricky tips: If you want to add some grass on top of the cookies, place some shredded coconut in a bag with a few drops of green food coloring. Shake until the coconut turns green.

HOW IT WORKS

Bedrock is the hard, solid rock beneath the soil. Common types of bedrock are granite and limestone. Subsoil is mostly made of weathered rocks and clay materials. It contains a lot of minerals for plant roots. Topsoil is a few feet deep and contains a lot of organic matter that is helpful in the germination, or the beginning of growth, of seeds. It contains bacteria, fungi, decay, and moisture.

MY SCIENTIST LIKED

_____

_____

_____

Fun with Yeast

Have you ever wondered how pizza gets its crispy, airy crust? Make your own pizza dough with yeast and watch what happens!

Science Question What does yeast do?

MESSY METER: 5

TIME NEEDED: 20 minutes prep, plus 60 to 90 minutes rising time and 20 minutes cooking time

ALLERGY ALERT: Gluten

WHAT YOU NEED

Dry measuring cup

1 cup all-purpose flour, plus more for dusting

2 large bowls

1 packet (7 grams) instant yeast

1½ teaspoons granulated sugar

¾ teaspoon table salt

Spoon for mixing

Measuring spoons

2 tablespoons olive oil, plus more for greasing

Liquid measuring cup

¾ cup warm water, plus more as needed

Paper towels (optional)

Plastic wrap

Pizza pan

Pizza toppings (sauce, cheese, pepperoni, vegetables, etc.)

1. Measure out 1 cup of flour. Put it in one of the large bowls. Repeat with the yeast, sugar, and salt, adding them on top of the flour. Stir until combined.

2. Measure out 2 tablespoons of olive oil. Add it to the bowl of flour. Measure out ¾ cup of warm water, and add it to the bowl, too. Stir well, until the mixture comes together to form a shaggy dough.

3. Gradually add more water, a tablespoon at a time, until the dough is slightly sticky.

4. Pour a little olive oil into the second large bowl and, using a paper towel or your hands, spread it all over to grease the bowl.

5. Put some flour on your hands and a clean work surface. Turn the dough out of the bowl and onto your floured work surface. Using your hands, knead the dough until it is soft and smooth. Form the dough into a ball. Place the ball in your greased bowl. Cover the bowl tightly with plastic wrap.

6. Set the bowl aside for 60 to 90 minutes to allow the dough to rise to double its size. While you are waiting, grease the pizza pan, similarly to how you greased the bowl in step 4.

7. Preheat the oven to 425°F. Meanwhile, transfer the dough to your pizza pan. Using your hands, work it into an even circle, pushing it right to the edge of the pizza pan.

8. Now it's time to make your pizza! You can dress your pizza with any of your favorite toppings. **Just for adults:** Carefully put the pan in the oven. Bake the pizza for 15 to 20 minutes, until the crust is cooked through and slightly browned and the cheese is melted.

continued ›

SPECIAL TIPS

Prep ahead: You will need at least 2 hours for this activity. The dough requires at least an hour to rise.

Fun together: Once you have shaped the dough and put it into the bowl, check on it every 15 minutes to see its progress. Use a ruler to measure how tall the ball of dough is before putting it in the bowl to rest, and then measure it again after. How many inches did it rise?

Tricky tips: If the dough gets too sticky, gradually work in more flour, a tablespoon at a time, until it's easy to work with.

HOW IT WORKS

Yeast makes dough rise—it's what is called a "leavening agent." The yeast feeds on the sugars in the dough and then turns the sugar into carbon dioxide. The carbon dioxide creates little air pockets in the dough. These air pockets increase the volume of the dough, which makes it rise.

MY SCIENTIST LIKED

_____

_____

_____

Edible Stained Glass

Make your own eye-catching stained-glass shapes by melting hard candy inside cookie cutters. These translucent shapes can be hung in your window for everyone to enjoy!

Science Question What happens when you put hard candy in the oven?

MESSY METER: 2

TIME NEEDED: 15 minutes

ALLERGY ALERT: None

WHAT YOU NEED

Hard candy or lollipops in several different colors

Resealable plastic sandwich bags

Mallet or small hammer

Baking sheet

Cooking spray

Metal cookie cutters

Pencil

String

1. Sort the candy by color. Set aside some candy to taste after the experiment. Put each color in a resealable bag, being careful to squish the air out of each bag, and seal. Place each candy bag in a second bag so the candy is double-bagged.

2. Time to use your muscles! Using a mallet or small hammer, crush the candy into small pieces.

3. Spray a baking sheet with cooking spray. Preheat the oven to 350°F.

4. Place metal cookie cutters on the baking sheet with their flat sides down. Now fill each cutter with different colors of crushed candy, mixing the colors however you like.

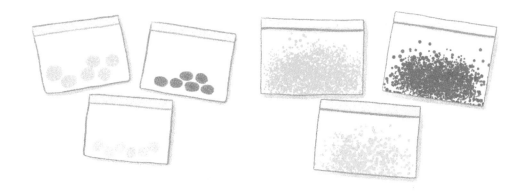

5.   **Just for adults:** Place the baking sheet in the preheated oven and bake the crushed candy for about 5 minutes, until melted.

6.   **Just for adults:** Remove the pan from the oven and let the candy cool for about 2 minutes. Then, using a pencil, poke a hole right through the candy. (This is where you will add a string to use as a hanger.) Set the candy aside to cool completely.

7.   Using your hands, carefully pop the candy out of the cookie cutters. Put a string through the hole, tie a knot, and hang the "stained glass" in a window.

continued ›

Fun together: Choose primary colors for your candy: red, yellow, and blue. When they melt together, they will make the secondary colors: orange, green, and purple.

Tricky tips: Don't keep the candy in the oven for too long or it will start to leak out of the bottoms of the cookie cutters. Let the candy cool completely before touching it. Don't use too much candy or it will be too thick for light to shine through.

HOW IT WORKS

When hard candy is heated in the oven, it melts and the colors mix together. The melted candy is thinner than the original piece of candy and becomes translucent, which makes it easier for light to pass through.

MY SCIENTIST LIKED

_____

_____

_____

Oobleck

Sometimes, science can get messy! Explore how this non-Newtonian fluid reacts when you touch it in different ways.

Science Question Can something be both a solid and a liquid?

MESSY METER: 5

TIME NEEDED: 15 minutes

ALLERGY ALERT: None

WHAT YOU NEED

2 cups cornstarch

1 cup water

Food coloring (red, yellow, blue)

Small mixing bowl

Shallow bowl, plate, or plastic tray

Spoon

Toothpick

1. Add 2 cups of cornstarch to a small mixing bowl. Put a little cornstarch on your finger. What does it taste like?

2. Slowly add water to the bowl. Let your child mix the cornstarch and water with a spoon. When it becomes too difficult to mix, you can begin to use your hands!

3. Continue to mix the ingredients, adding more water or cornstarch as necessary. The consistency should feel gooey.

4. Pour the oobleck into a shallow bowl, plate, or plastic tray. Add 2 drops of red, yellow, and blue food coloring.

5. Use a toothpick to slowly swirl the colors.

6. Once the colors are well mixed, enjoy playing with and exploring the oobleck with your hands.

Fun together: What happens if you tap the oobleck quickly with your finger? What happens if you slowly press your finger into it? Can you roll it into a ball with your hands?   Pick some up with your hands and let go. Watch what happens!

Tricky tips: The oobleck will be difficult to mix. Try using your hands to slowly mix in the water and cornstarch until it's well combined. If you want to make your oobleck all one color instead of mixing food coloring, add 10 drops of food coloring to the water before you add it to the cornstarch.

HOW IT WORKS

Oobleck is a non-Newtonian fluid. When cornstarch mixes with water, the starch doesn't dissolve. If you move the mixture slowly, the particles in the cornstarch move past each other and act like a liquid. If you move it quickly, the particles in the cornstarch become twisted with each other, causing it to act like a solid.

MY SCIENTIST LIKED

_____

_____

_____

Quick-Freeze Sorbet

Turn juice into sorbet while investigating how adding salt to ice causes a liquid to freeze faster.

Science Question What happens to ice when you add salt?

MESSY METER: 2

TIME NEEDED: 10 minutes

ALLERGY ALERT: None

WHAT YOU NEED

Liquid measuring cup

1 cup fruit juice

1 resealable sandwich bag

Ice cubes

1 resealable
half-gallon-size bag

Dry measuring cup

¼ cup table salt

Towel

Bowl

Spoon

1. Using the liquid measuring cup, measure out 1 cup of juice. Pour it into a resealable sandwich bag. Squeeze out any air and seal the bag.

2. Add ice to the half-gallon resealable bag until it is about half full.

3. Using the dry measuring cup, measure out ¼ cup of salt. Add it to the bag of ice. Seal and shake the bag to distribute the salt well.

4. Now, place your sealed bag of juice in the middle of the ice. Press out the air and seal the bag of ice.

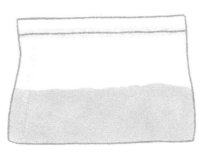

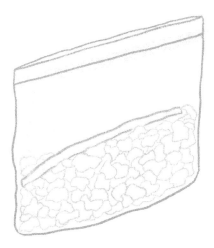

5. Place a towel over the bag and gently massage the ice so that it's constantly in contact with the bag of juice.

6. After 5 minutes, open the bag of ice and take out your bag of delicious fruit sorbet.

7. Now it's time to eat your experiment! Pour the sorbet into a serving bowl and eat it with a spoon.

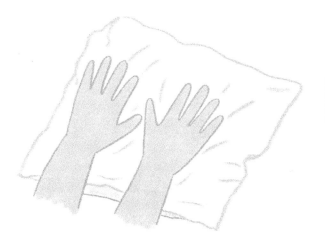
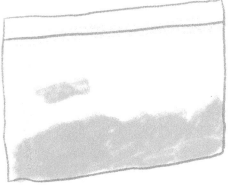

continued ›

SPECIAL TIPS

Fun together: Give your child the bag with salt and ice while you do the same activity with a bag that has only ice (no salt added). Race each other to see whose juice turns to sorbet first!

Tricky tips: You may want to place another half-gallon bag over the one containing the ice to prevent the ice from tearing the bag and leaking.

HOW IT WORKS

When salt is added to ice, it lowers its freezing point. The ice wants to melt, so it tries to take the heat from the juice. When heat moves from the juice to the ice, the juice freezes faster.

MY SCIENTIST LIKED

_____

_____

_____

Measurement Conversions

Volume Equivalents	U.S. Standard	U.S. Standard (ounces)	Metric (approximate)
Liquid	2 tablespoons	1 fl. oz.	30 mL
	¼ cup	2 fl. oz.	60 mL
	½ cup	4 fl. oz.	120 mL
	1 cup	8 fl. oz.	240 mL
	1½ cups	12 fl. oz.	355 mL
	2 cups or 1 pint	16 fl. oz.	475 mL
	4 cups or 1 quart	32 fl. oz.	1 L
	1 gallon	128 fl. oz.	4 L
Dry	⅛ teaspoon		0.5 mL
	¼ teaspoon		1 mL
	½ teaspoon		2 mL
	¾ teaspoon		4 mL
	1 teaspoon		5 mL
	1 tablespoon		15 mL
	¼ cup		59 mL
	⅓ cup		79 mL
	½ cup		118 mL
	⅔ cup		156 mL
	¾ cup		177 mL
	1 cup		235 mL
	2 cups or 1 pint		475 mL
	3 cups		700 mL
	4 cups or 1 quart		1 L
	½ gallon		2 L
	1 gallon		4 L

Oven Temperatures

Fahrenheit	Celsius (approximate)
250°F	120°C
300°F	150°C
325°F	165°C
350°F	180°C
375°F	190°C
400°F	200°C
425°F	220°C
450°F	230°C

Weight Equivalents

U.S. Standard	Metric (approximate)
½ ounce	15 g
1 ounce	30 g
2 ounces	60 g
4 ounces	115 g
8 ounces	225 g
12 ounces	340 g
16 ounces or 1 pound	455 g

Resources

Websites:

Science Sparks, Science-Sparks.com

Little Bins for Little Hands, LittleBinsForLittleHands.com

The Dad Lab, TheDabLab.com

Go Science Kids, GoScienceKids.com

Toddler Approved, ToddlerApproved.com

Books:

Big Science for Little People: 52 Activities to Help You & Your Child Discover the Wonders of Science by Lynn Brunelle

STEAM Play & Learn: 20 Fun Step-by-Step Preschool Projects About Science, Technology, Engineering, Art, and Math! by Ana Dziengel

The Curious Kid's Science Book: 100+ Creative Hands-On Activities for Ages 4-8 by Asia Citro

Preschool Hands-On STEAM Learning Fun Workbook, Highlights Learning Fun Workbooks

Index

Acknowledgments

I would like to gratefully extend my appreciation to my husband, Greg, for being my biggest supporter in life, my family and friends who encouraged and stood by me as I took a giant leap into starting my own education business, and my daughters, Amelia and Julia, for helping me test out ideas for this book. Thank you to Callisto Media for providing me with the wonderful opportunity to bring hands-on science activities into the homes of so many families!

About the Author

 Melissa Mazur is an educator with experience in both third- and fifth-grade general education as well as preschool science. She holds a master's degree in educational technology and specialized teaching endorsements in science, language arts, social studies, and middle-school education. Mazur has a passion for education. She became inspired to challenge and stimulate students by introducing project-based learning experiences into the curriculum.

In addition to teaching in the classroom, Mazur is an educational blogger and curriculum designer. Through her company Learning Lab Resources, she has spent years writing, creating, and developing educational resources and curriculum for teachers. It is her goal to provide both teachers and students with engaging ideas and materials to help make learning meaningful.

About the Illustrator

 Natascha Rosenberg is an illustrator and writer of picture books for kids and for older people who continue to enjoy children's books. She has created illustrations for books, magazines, and toys, and her books have been published in Europe, the USA, and Asia. Rosenberg is the author of *Valentina* and *El Viaje de Lea*, among others, published in Spain by SM Ediciones and selected at the International Book Fair of Bologna in 2014. You can see more of her work on her website NataschaRosenberg.com.

CPSIA information can be obtained
at www.ICGtesting.com
Printed in the USA
JSHW041116061121
20176JS00004B/4

9 781638 071143